One Story

By
Ethan Longhenry

© 2023 Spiritbuilding Publishers.
All rights reserved. No part of this book may be reproduced in any form without the written permission of the publisher.

Published by
Spiritbuilding Publishers
9700 Ferry Road, Waynesville, Ohio 45068

ONE STORY
By Ethan Longhenry

ISBN: 978-1955285-78-0

Spiritbuilding
PUBLISHERS

spiritbuilding.com

Table of Contents

Introduction 1

ONE God 3

ONE Man 14

ONE Another 29

ONE Story 40

Your Role in the ONE Story 56

Introduction

E PLURIBUS UNUM
(out of many, one; on the Seal of the United States)

One love / one blood / one life /you got to do what you should
One life / with each other /sisters / brothers
One life / but we're not the same
We get to / carry each other (U2, One)

> I do not ask for these only, but also for those who will
> believe in me through their word, that they may all be one,
> just as you, Father, are in me, and I in you, that they also may
> be in us, so that the world may believe that you have sent me.
> —Jesus, John 17:20–21

What are we looking for out of life?

What is our goal in our relationships with one another?

How can we find the harmony in life we so desperately seek?

We have heard many answers coming from many different time periods and perspectives. So, who should we trust and believe?

We can find a way forward regarding these questions by seeking after true unity: to be ONE.

ONE begins with the 'One God'. Who is God? How can we know anything about Him? What is our relationship with Him? Where is He?

We then must factor in the 'One Man'. Who is this Man? Why is He important? Why should we listen to Him? What role did this One man plan in correcting what went wrong between God and humankind?

Then we must turn to 'One Another.' What kind of relationship should we have with one another? How can we achieve that relationship? How does this relate to the One God and the One Man?

Let us begin our study of these major issues that we all face in our lives so that we may be One with God and with one another, sharing together in God's ONE story!

ONE God

> "Hear, O Israel: YHWH our God, YHWH is one."
> —Moses, Deuteronomy 6:4

> "I and the Father are one."
> —Jesus, John 10:30

> "And [God] made from one man every nation of mankind to live on all the face of the earth, having determined allotted periods and the boundaries of their dwelling place, that they should seek God, in the hope that they might feel their way toward him and find him. Yet he is actually not far from each one of us, for 'In him we live and move and have our being'; as even some of your own poets have said, 'For we are indeed his offspring.'"
> —Paul, Acts 17:26–28

We start at the beginning, and in the beginning, there was God, according to Genesis 1:1. Everything we will discover about unity and the One will find its origin and basis in God.

Who is God?

As we begin this study, let us seek to understand the picture of God as presented within the pages of the Bible. Perhaps you are here and are not completely sold on the idea that the Bible is God's revelation to humans. For now, if that's the case, I ask you to keep an open mind to the material, and give it an honest hearing. Hopefully, it will show how the Bible's picture of God makes sense in terms of the reality which we experience.

God is spoken of as the Creator of the heavens and the earth (Genesis 1:1—2:3). According to Colossians 1:17 and Hebrews 1:3, all things consist in God, and God continues to uphold and sustain the universe by His power.

Jesus declares that God is spirit (John 4:24). We are not told much about the nature of spiritual beings, but we do know God has personality; He is not an "it," a "thing," or some vague mist or vapor or any such thing.

Above all, the Bible makes it known that God is all-powerful, all-knowing, and all-present (cf. Job 28:24, Psalm 147:5, Acts 17:26-27, Hebrews 4:13, Revelation 19:6). His personal name—YHWH, most likely pronounced Yahweh—simply means I AM, or the "Existent One" (cf. Exodus 3:14). We live and move and have our being within God. In this view, if there is no God, there is nothing at all.

If we understand that God is our Creator, the Author and Giver of life, and all-powerful, then we should understand we are not all-knowing or all-powerful. As we continue in our discussions, it is important for us to keep two passages in mind:

'"For my thoughts are not your thoughts, neither are your ways my ways," declares YHWH. "For as the heavens are higher than the earth, so are my ways higher than your ways and my thoughts than your thoughts."' (Isaiah 55:8-9)

"The secret things belong to YHWH our God, but the things that are revealed belong to us and to our children forever, that we may do all the words of this law." (Moses, Deuteronomy 29:29)

There are some questions whose answers we cannot understand. Some aspects of God, His nature, and His work are beyond our capabilities. Nevertheless, the Bible indicates that God has made many revelations regarding Himself to humans, and humans are expected to understand those revelations. Therefore, we must be careful: we must not go beyond what we can know, but we must work to come to an understanding of what can be known.

The Father, the Son, and the Holy Spirit

According to the Bible, God is the Creator, a Spirit, all-knowing, all-present, and all-powerful. He has revealed some things about Himself to people, and there are other things about Him which people cannot understand. Since God is so great, why do we exist? Why would God bother to create this universe and to have anything to do with us humans?

For us to explore this question further, we must dig deeper into an understanding of who God is. From the days of Moses on, one of the great declarations about God is that He is One. (Deuteronomy 6:4) In a world where most people believed in many different gods controlling different aspects of this world, the idea that there was really just one God behind everything was radical and controversial!

But how is God one? A lot of people just assume that God is one like you are one and I am one: one person. But let us look at what the Bible says:

- "In the beginning was the Word, and the Word was with God, and the Word was God." (John, John 1:1)
- 'Jesus said to them, "Truly, truly, I say to you, before Abraham was, I am."' (John 8:58)
- "For in [Jesus] the whole fullness of deity dwells bodily." (Paul, Colossians 2:9)
- "Peter, an apostle of Jesus Christ, to those who are elect exiles of the dispersion in Pontus, Galatia, Cappadocia, Asia, and Bithynia, according to the foreknowledge of God the Father, in the sanctification of the Spirit, for obedience to Jesus Christ and for sprinkling with his blood: May grace and peace be multiplied to you." (1 Peter 1:1–2)
- "For no prophecy was ever produced by the will of man, but men spoke from God as they were carried along by the Holy Spirit." (2 Peter 1:21)

We learn in Deuteronomy 6:4 that God is One, but when we look at these passages, it seems that Jesus, John, Paul, and Peter are saying that the Word, Jesus, is also God, and the Holy Spirit is God as well. How can this be?

There are only three possible answers. The first is to say that God remains one person but has three forms: God as the Father, God as the Son, Jesus, or God as the Holy Spirit. But the Bible shows that this view does not work: all three are present when Jesus is baptized in Matthew 3:16-17, and Jesus declares that the Father and the Son are two separate witnesses in John 8:17-18. The second is to say that God the Father is really God, and while Jesus and the Spirit are divine, they are not on the same level of divinity as God the Father. Yet the Bible again speaks differently: notice how Paul says that the fullness of the Godhead dwells in Jesus in Colossians 2:9, and John says that the Word was not just with God but was also God in John 1:1.

Notice how both answers try to maintain the assumption that God is one in person. Yet no passage of Scripture declares that God is one Person. This brings us to our third answer: The Father, the Son, and the Holy Spirit are all one God, but in three Persons. This is the idea of the Trinity, or the Triune God. Despite all the bad press this idea receives, it remains the best way to try to understand how God is One yet Three.

Yes, we have now ventured deeply into the dark forest of theology. Theology is often understood as boring and mostly irrelevant to life. This is a sad reputation, especially considering how important the Triune God is to our understanding of the world in which we live. It is only when we understand how God is One in Three that we can really understand why He bothered to create the universe and us in it.

How, therefore, can God be considered One yet in Three Persons? While much remains mysterious, and beyond our understanding, the Bible does tell us some things about this unity. God is one in eternal existence: as John says, the Word was God and with God from before the beginning (John 1:1-3), and the Spirit was there as well (Genesis 1:2). This means that all three are One in "age". God is also of the same substance, or being; the Father is spirit, the Word is spirit, and the Spirit, obviously, is spirit (John 1:14, 4:24). We will see in the future that the Word, otherwise known as Jesus, or the Son, will take on human flesh, but that does not change the fact that He remained fully God and thus spirit. God is of the same character: all the qualities that mark the Father are also true of the Word/Son and Spirit (Hebrews 1:3). God also has one will: the Father, the Word/Son, and Spirit all have the same purpose, ideas, and intentions (cf. John 17:20-23).

We could get into a lot more detail about what can be known about the inner workings of the nature of God, but ultimately, God wants us to understand that He is One in 'relational unity'. God is One in Three Persons because of the powerful relationship that exists amongst the Three!

Jesus provides a glimpse of this in John 17:20-23:
> I do not ask for these only, but also for those who will believe in me through their word, that they may all be one, just as you, Father, are in me, and I in you, that they also may be in us, so that the world may believe that you have sent me. The glory that you have given me I have given to them, that they may be one even as we are one, I in them and you in me, that they may become perfectly one, so that the world may know that you sent me and loved them even as you loved me.

The Father is in the Son and the Son is in the Father; they are perfectly One, and yet they remain distinct Persons. The same is true with the Spirit. Their unity is not based in personhood but in *relationship*. Think about it: God is so perfectly unified in nature and will that we can speak of Him in the singular. Even though it is

God the Father, God the Word/Son, and God the Holy Spirit, God is One. He is YHWH, the Existent One: the Father, the Word/Son, and the Holy Spirit, all perfectly One.

What Does It All Mean?

So God is One according to relational unity. Why does that matter? And how can we know for sure?

We have wanted to know why God bothered to create the world and to have anything to do with us. Jesus really gives us an answer to those questions in John 17:20–23, but we first need to consider a few big issues.

The Bible declares that God is love in 1 John 4:8. Defining love can get tricky in society today, but both the Greek word and its use in the Bible shows us that love involves seeking the best interest of the beloved, even at great personal cost (cf. John 3:16, 1 Corinthians 13:4–8, 1 John 4:7–21). Love is something that can only exist within some sort of a relationship; therefore, this is a strong proof that God is one in relational unity, since He would have to be in relationship within Himself to be love.

Likewise, the Bible declares that God can be known not just through what He has spoken to people but also through the creation. Paul says that God's invisible attributes—His eternal power and His divine nature—can be perceived in the creation that He made. (Romans 1:19–20) To this day we are left awestruck at the majesty of creation, and how everything works together to facilitate life: everything from constants of the operation of the universe down to the coding of DNA. We can therefore see God's eternal power. But where do we perceive God's divine nature?

This brings us to the third great declaration of Scripture: man is made in God's image.

Then God said, "Let us make man in our image, after our likeness. And let them have dominion over the fish of the sea and over the birds of the heavens and over the livestock and over all the earth and over every creeping thing that creeps on the earth." So God created man in his own image, in the image of God he created him; male and female he created them (Genesis 1:26–27).

For, 'In [God] we live and move and have our being'; as even some of your own poets have said, 'For we are indeed his offspring.' Being then God's offspring, we ought not to think that the divine being is like gold or silver or stone, an image formed by the art and imagination of man (Paul, Acts 17:28–29).

Since God is not physical but spiritual, we can safely declare that God is not a human (John 4:24). Thus, if we are made in God's image, it has something to do with our minds, hearts, and souls!

What are we all looking for in life? While it is true that different people are motivated by different ideals and purposes, most of us really seek after the same things. We might want a comfortable lifestyle, money, and such things, but we cannot imagine having those things alone. Many people want to be as wealthy as Ebenezer Scrooge, but no one really wants to be Ebenezer Scrooge! We want to have connections with other people. We seek after that one special person with whom we will maintain close intimacy, physically and emotionally. We seek to be known, to be loved, and to be appreciated. In short, we seek 'relationships'. In fact, scientists and psychologists are discovering that we humans are wired to be social animals: we were not designed to be isolated from each other. We want to share in relationships!

Let's stop and think about the relationship we normally associate with the term: marriage. What is the ideal situation? We have one man and one woman who are not related to each other. Through one of a few processes, they meet, get to know each other, and create a deep connection. They make a commitment to each other because of their love for one another. Even though they remain two individual people, they become one: they are one in being (they're both humans), they work to share one will, and they seek each other's best interest. It is no longer about "me" for either of them; it becomes about "us."

What is the result when these two become one? They want to share in that love, not just with one another, but in a product of that relationship. Children are born and raised with the expectation that there will remain a sense of oneness in relationship within the family. Yes, the children will likely grow up and marry spouses themselves, but ideally, parents and children still share in life together at some level. They still remain one family, even as it grows with grandchildren and great-grandchildren and so on and so forth.

None of this is coincidental. Genesis 2:18, 24 says, 'Then YHWH God said, "It is not good that the man should be alone; I will make him a helper fit for him." … "Therefore a man shall leave his father and his mother and hold fast to his wife, and they shall become one flesh."

It is not good for man to be alone because man was never made to be alone. Man could never have been made to be alone because he was made in God's image, and who is God but Three Persons in relational unity? Man was made for relationship, for God is one in the relationship.

In marriage, the two become one, just as the Father, the Son, and the Spirit are one.

Let us consider again John 17:20-23 (emphasis mine):

> I do not ask for these only, but also for those who will believe in me through their word, **that they may all be one,**

just as you, Father, are in me, and I in you, that they also may be in us, so that the world may believe that you have sent me. The glory that you have given me I have given to them, **that they may be one even as we are one, I in them and you in me, that they may become perfectly one**, so that the world may know that you sent me and loved them even as you loved me.

The Father, the Son, and the Holy Spirit are One. Therefore, God, I, and my fellow man are to be one. This does not mean that humans become gods, but it does mean that humans are to better reflect the image of God. This is the way God has always intended.

We now have our answers. God is love, and God shared in that love within Himself. Thus, God is so relationally one that we can speak of Him in the singular, even though God is in Three Persons. We can understand this in part from the analogy of marriage.

And just as love in marriage ideally leads to a desire to share that love with offspring, so God as love wanted to share that love with "offspring"—the creation, this universe, and this world—and especially with those creatures made in God's image, humanity. God wants to have a deep, close relationship with humans, to share in the joy of true, self-sacrificial love. And just as true love cannot be forced, so God does not force that relationship on anyone. Instead, He invites people to share in that relationship.

Is there a God? And is that God the Triune God revealed in the pages of the Bible? Let's look around. Can we not perceive that there is a power greater than ourselves, an intelligent, creative being who can appreciate aesthetic pleasures such as art and beauty? Don't we appreciate beauty and creativity? Do we seek after meaning, connection, relationship, and love? Don't we get the impression that there is something more to life than just the biological realities of living? Why do we seek meaning if meaning is just a tragic misfiring of our biological development? And why is it that we are still nagged with this understanding, deep down, that there are such things as right and wrong, and that justice is worth pursuing?

Why are we all so afraid of being left alone and abandoned?

Paul is right. There is a God, and His eternal power and divine nature can be perceived in the physical universe and within the design of humanity made in His image. It makes sense to believe that God is love and that all things exist on account of that love. It makes sense that God is Three in One, maintaining relational unity, since humans seek relationship, not just with fellow humans but also with his environment and his Creator. It is not good for us to be alone. We need a relationship with our Creator.

Nevertheless, as we look around, we see a lot of pain, suffering, abuse, hatred, and discord. Things are not all lovely around here. What happened? How can it be made better? These will be our subjects as we consider the ONE Man in our next lesson.

Questions for Discussion

1. Who is God?

2. How can God be One in Three Persons?

3. How does the creation show us that there is a God?

4. How does the creation show us that God is One in relational unity?

5. What does it mean that humans are made in God's image?

6. How can we know that man is made in God's image?

7. Why did God create the universe?

8. Why are we here?

ONE Man

Therefore, just as sin came into the world through one man, and death through sin, and so death spread to all men because all sinned (Romans 5:12).

For by works of the law no human being will be justified in his sight, since through the law comes knowledge of sin (Romans 3:20).

For while we were still weak, at the right time Christ died for the ungodly. For one will scarcely die for a righteous person: though perhaps for a good person one would dare even to die; but God shows his love for us in that while we were still sinners, Christ died for us. Since, therefore, we have now been justified by his blood, much more shall we be saved by him from the wrath of God. For if while we were enemies we were reconciled to God by the death of his Son, much more, now that we are reconciled, shall we be saved by his life (Romans 5:6–10).

For those whom he foreknew he also predestined to be conformed to the image of his Son, in order that he might be the firstborn among many brothers (Romans 8:29).

We have learned some things about God: He is the Triune God, the Three in One, loving in relational unity. On account of that great love, He created all things and seeks relationship with us. It sounds so wonderful, so what has gone so wrong?

Understanding the Problem

We look around and the problem seems pretty clear to us: things do not work perfectly. Animals, plants, and other creatures die.

Objects corrode, decay, or rust. There is a lot of violence around, both naturally and because of humans. We see plenty of misery about: pain, suffering, sickness, and death. None of this seems very good; none of this seems to correspond with the beautiful picture of Creation in Genesis 1:1–2:3.

The problem stems from sin. Sin can be understood in different ways. In one sense, sin is "missing the mark," for it involves conduct not living up to the standard. In another sense, sin is transgression, for it goes against God's purposes for the world. Sin is also rightly understood as rebellion, since it represents a conscious rejection of God's ways for one's own ways.

When God made the first man and woman, He gave them one commandment: do not eat of the fruit of the tree of the knowledge of good and evil (Genesis 2:16–17). They did not follow that one commandment, but instead ate of that fruit and so transgressed (Genesis 3:1–19); that transgression was the first sin, and by it sin and death entered the world, as Paul describes in Romans 5:12–19.

It is important for us to understand what happened when Adam and Eve sinned. Their transgression had personal consequences, as we shall see, but the whole creation suffered because of it. Paul will speak in Romans 8:19–25 of the fact that the creation was "subjected to futility" and is in "bondage to corruption." This began with the sin of Adam and Eve. This is why things decay in the universe; this is why suffering extends not just to people who have intentionally sinned but also to animals and innocent humans.

Yet, the most terrible consequence of Adam and Eve's transgression was their subsequent separation from God. This was first marked physically: they were cast out of the Garden, forced to work the now cursed ground (Genesis 3:22–24). While it is true Adam and Eve did not physically die on that day, they began the process of dying: the consequence of their separation from God. This is why it is written, "But your iniquities have made a separation between you and your God, and your sins have hidden his face from you so that he does not hear" (Isaiah 59:2).

Sin separates humans from God. The consequence of sin is that people are separated from the Source of light and life, and what is death but separation from life? Humans first experience this spiritually, and then, sadly, physically as well.

How could God let this happen? Did He not create us to enjoy relationship with Him, but now He has allowed sin to infect that relationship? We must be careful as we explore these questions. As we have said, God is love (1 John 4:8), and a hallmark of love is that it does not insist on its own way (cf. 1 Corinthians 13:5). God created us in an act of love so that we might learn to love Him; such love cannot be forced on either end. If God compels or coerces us, He no longer is acting in love; likewise, if we had no choice but to love God, it is no longer love as we know it. For us to be able to love we must have the choice to not love; for us to be able to follow God, we must have the choice to not follow God. That is why God made the command in the Garden but did not force Adam and Eve to follow it; and so it is to this day.

So, what happens because of this separation? God still loves people who are separated from Him; He still acts kindly toward them (Matthew 5:45–47). Unfortunately, this separation grows ever more pronounced since mankind continues in rebellion. Left to his own devices, mankind will wander off into various false ideas; he will perceive that there is something beyond himself but will not be able to accurately identify it. Far too often he will make up a god or gods of his own choosing, be it himself, his abilities, natural forces, physical impulses, or some such thing (cf. Romans 1:18–25). While mankind remains in this condition, he cannot serve God, but is hostile toward Him and His truth (Romans 8:7–8). The image of God is still there in mankind, but it becomes ever more distorted the more and more he rebels against God and transgresses His purposes.

This process is illustrated in man's early history as revealed in the Bible. After a few generations, people were so sinful God decided to cause all to perish except Noah and his family in a flood (Genesis 4-9). After the Flood, man tried to build a tower all the way to heaven to make a name for themselves, and God felt compelled to scatter them and confuse their language (Genesis 10-11). Most people wandered far from God; God would choose one person— Abraham—and Isaac, and Jacob through him (Genesis 12-51). Yet even Israel's history is full of transgression against God, leading to exile away from the land God gave them (Joshua-2 Chronicles). Sin multiplies as time progresses.

If a person dies, still separated from God, he will remain in that condition forever (Romans 2:5-11). That sounds harsh to a lot of people. Many cannot tolerate the idea that there is a place people go where they are eternally separated from God and light and life: hell (2 Thessalonians 1:6-9). But do we remember that God loves everyone, and love cannot be forced? How can God be truly loving if He forces people who are separated from Him and have not indicated they want a relationship with Him to have that relationship eternally? God will not be actively condemning them; God is giving them over to what they have always demonstrably wanted by their words and/or deeds. They will remain separated from Him for eternity, just as they have wanted.

Sin, therefore, is the problem. It disfigures mankind, it disfigures the creation, and we all see the pain, suffering, and misery that it causes. So, what can be done about it?

Our Solution Problem

We humans are good problem solvers. When we are made aware of a problem, we want to figure out how to fix it. But the sin problem leads to a solution problem: we cannot do anything about it!

This also may sound harsh. Can we not just make up for our sins by doing good things? We would like to think so: we like the image of the balancing scales, and the idea that if our sins are fewer than our good deeds, we will make it in the end.

Unfortunately, we humans have been tainted with sin. This means that a lot of the ideas we have are not really accurate or good in the eyes of God. We do well to heed the warning of those who have come before us:

- Proverbs 3:5–6—"Trust in YHWH with all your heart, and do not lean on your own understanding. In all your ways acknowledge him, and he will make straight your paths."
- Proverbs 14:12—"There is a way that seems right to a man, but its end is the way to death."
- Jeremiah 10:23—"I know, O YHWH, that the way of man is not in himself, that it is not in man who walks to direct his steps."

We must never trust any idea because we like it or because it makes sense to us. We do better to trust in God our Creator and hear what He has to say.

We have spoken about how God is love, and that is true (1 John 4:8). But God is also a God of justice (Psalm 33:5, 37:28). The Psalmist declares that righteousness and justice are the foundations of God's throne (Psalm 9:7, 89:14). We should not imagine that God has some physical throne somewhere; the Psalmist means that God's authority in this universe is founded upon His righteousness and justice.

Remember how we spoke about God's eternal power and divine nature being seen in His creation from Romans 1:19–20? So it is here with justice and righteousness. While every culture and society have different rules and regulations, is it not interesting that there is a universal understanding that murder, adultery, and stealing are "wrong"? Recent studies have shown that children have a sense of "right" and "wrong" as infants. Where did these ideas of "right" and "wrong" come from? Why is it that we feel "wronged" if someone steals from us or violates us in some way? We all have a "moral law" within us, no matter how some may deny that it is there. That "moral law" is a powerful testimony regarding the existence of God: and it also testifies to His standard of justice.

The precise definition of justice has been argued about for 2,500 years, but its basic idea is clear: justice is the demand that wrong behavior be punished, and right behavior be honored. We believe it just, or fair, for people who do good things to be honored and rewarded for it. We also believe it just, or fair, for people who do bad things to pay a penalty for doing so.

God is just and righteous; His power is rooted in justice and righteousness. This is why God made known to mankind the guidelines of behavior that are right: so we, as God's creation made in His image, could understand what righteousness is. This standard is not just some arbitrary list of "thou shalts" and "thou shalt nots." When God reveals what is right from wrong, God is revealing how we can live in harmony with Him and His creation, and, by extension, how we live in disharmony with Him and His creation. If we do what God says to do, and do not do what God says not to do, we would be righteous and live in complete harmony with Him and His creation. When we do what God says not to do, or do not do what He tells us to do, then we are in rebellion against Him and the way He composed the universe. Little wonder, then, that there are so many environmental consequences for sin: the consequences of sin do not just impact people, but the creation as well!

God is a God of justice: therefore, there must be some penalty paid for wrong behavior. That is why the "wages of sin is death" as Paul says in Romans 6:23; when we sin, the penalty for that sin is death. We suffer the consequence for our conduct.

But what about all of our good deeds? Do they matter?

'For whoever keeps the whole law but fails in one point has become accountable for all of it. For he who said, "Do not commit adultery," also said, "Do not murder." If you do not commit adultery but do murder, you have become a transgressor of the law' (James 2:10–11).

What is James saying? Let us imagine a courtroom. You are on trial for stealing. Your defense lawyer, declares the following, "The defendant admits to stealing. But I would have you know that the defendant has not murdered anyone, has not committed adultery, has helped a lot of poor people in need, and is very kind."
What would you think of that defense? It is no defense at all! The judge or jury will convict you for stealing. It does not matter how many other things you have not done, nor does it matter what other things you have done. If you have transgressed the law, you are a transgressor, plain and simple. And if justice is going to be served, you are going to have to pay the penalty.

That is what James is saying, and that is why Paul declares in Romans 3:20 that no one will be justified—that is, declared righteous—by works of the law. There is no law standard we can appeal to and say that we have followed it perfectly. With one violation, we are declared transgressors: no matter how small or big, no matter how rarely or often. We have done bad things, and if justice will be served, a penalty must be paid.

As Paul declares, 'For all have sinned and fall short of the glory of God' (Romans 3:23).

We have all fallen short. We cannot, on our own, change that. We cannot, on our own, make it better. We find ourselves disfigured by sin, separated from God, far too often separated from each other, lonely, searching for something. What a sad condition!

The Solution: The ONE Man

Man finds himself separated from God on account of his transgressions. God cannot just arbitrarily remove the consequences of man's behavior if He will remain a God of justice. The penalty for sin *must* be paid.

But does each person have to pay that penalty and remain separated from God forever? There would be no point to this study if that were the case. Since God loves mankind and wants to maintain a relationship with them, and He understands that justice must be honored, He was willing to go to extraordinary lengths to bridge the divide and to allow for the reconciliation between Himself and His creation. He did this through the ONE Man.

The ONE Man, in the flesh, had humble beginnings. He was born to a peasant carpenter and his teenage wife in the back country of Galilee, itself considered the back country of Israel. He never went to school, yet even from His youth it was clear that He was not an ordinary person.

The ONE Man came to a man recognized as a prophet, a spokesman of God, named John the Baptist. John declared regarding the ONE Man that He was the "Lamb of God who takes away the sin of the world" (John 1:29). The ONE Man proved willing to be baptized by John, and the Holy Spirit descended upon Him as a dove, and the voice of the Father provided His approval: this ONE Man, Jesus of Nazareth, was God's Son, and God was well–pleased with Him (Matthew 3:16–17).

Jesus then suffered temptation at the hands of the Devil; whereas Adam sinned, Jesus did not. Jesus then went about Galilee, Judea, and other lands nearby over a space of three years. He taught the Israelites in profound ways, using imagery familiar to the farmers and fishermen around Him. Unlike the religious authorities of the day, Jesus taught them as one having authority. He taught them difficult things. Love your enemies. Do good to people who do not like you. Be willing to suffer humiliation. Humble yourselves. Perhaps the stranger thing was that He Himself did all the things He taught. He went about doing good, healing people, demonstrating God's power through Him.

This Jesus spoke constantly about a Kingdom that God would establish. He gathered around Himself twelve men, a motley crew of fishermen, tax collectors, revolutionaries, and other men of the lower class. The Kingdom of which He spoke was going to be radically different from anything people had ever seen before. Its rules and guidelines would turn the world upside down.

Even though Jesus went about doing good, He earned the ire of the religious authorities. They conspired to put Him to death, and at the time of the Passover feast around the year 30 CE, they accused Him, condemned Him, and handed Him over to the Roman authorities to kill Him. The Roman authorities did so, choosing the most violent and degrading form of execution ever invented by humans: crucifixion.

People thought that such would be the end of it; Jesus was not the first professed King to be killed on a Roman cross. But on the third day after His crucifixion, this Jesus did something that no one else before or since has ever done. He was resurrected from the dead in bodily form, never to die again. He spent some time with His followers and then ascended back to heaven, where the Father gave Him all rule and authority over heaven and earth. Soon after, those followers began telling all the Jews, and then other people as well, about this Jesus, how He died and rose again, and how God made Him YHWH, and that all people should serve Him. This message took the Roman world by storm. Nothing would be the same again.

This is the story of the ONE Man that can be found in the Gospels of Matthew, Mark, Luke, and John, and the early part of the book of Acts. The Apostle Paul and others would later tell people who believed in Jesus just how the ONE Man, Jesus, allowed us to be rescued from sin.

Adam and Eve's children sacrificed animals and produce to God (Genesis 4). This is based in man's attempt to pay the penalty for his sin. God would later make some of this clear in Leviticus. Bulls, goats, and sheep, at various times, would be sacrificed for sin. The animals were sacrificed because they were innocent, and the sins of the guilty person would be transferred to the animal through ritual.

Yet, as the Hebrew author would later declare, the blood of bulls and goats cannot take away sin (Hebrews 10:4). This whole sacrificial system was designed to teach people the ugliness of sin and the type of mechanism that was necessary if the penalty for sin would be covered, or atoned, by another.

This is why John called the ONE Man, Jesus, the "Lamb of God, who takes away the sin of the world." Jesus was innocent in life; He did not sin, even though He was tempted to do so (Hebrews 4:15). He did not deserve to die, but He died to pay the penalty for our sin (John 3:16, 2 Corinthians 5:21). As the perfect Man, He was the only one who could pay the penalty for our sin!

This one act of sacrifice was enough to pay the penalty for all sin: He is the perfect priest in offering up Himself once for all, as the Hebrew author says (Hebrews 7:23–28); as Paul says, as the first man Adam sinned once and sin spread to all men, so the second Adam, Jesus, paid the penalty once and allowed for redemption (Romans 5:12–19).

Therefore, God does through Jesus what people could not do for themselves. Jesus, the Son of God and God the Son, paid the penalty of sin for us. God's justice is satisfied; we describe this act as one of grace and mercy, since God gave us what was not deserved (grace) and did not give us what we did deserve (mercy). Through Jesus' death, we can receive forgiveness of sin. Through Jesus' resurrection, we can understand that death is not the end, and we can cherish the hope of our own resurrection one day (1 Corinthians 15).

We could not, by our own efforts, reconcile ourselves to God; God proves willing to reconcile us to Himself through the ONE Man Jesus, Son of God and God the Son (Romans 5:6–11). God be praised!

Restoring the Relationship

So, God has done what we could not do; through Jesus we can be reconciled to God and restored to Him.

Yet God does not compel or coerce; just as He did not force mankind into a relationship with Him at the beginning, so He does not force mankind into a relationship now. Access is offered; it is left to us to accept that access.

The message of the ONE Man went forth throughout the world, and people were invited to a restored relationship with God through Christ. Jesus is now ruling, and everyone will have to answer to Him (John 12:48, Acts 17:31). If people want a restored relationship with God, they will have to do so by following what Jesus has said.

Jesus gave authority to those twelve men, the apostles, to tell people about Him and what they needed to do to be rescued from their sin.

They declared that people must believe Jesus is the Son of God (Acts 16:31, Romans 10:9–10). This belief is more than just a profession of faith: it means that we are trusting in Jesus as YHWH (James 2:14–26). Those who believe this must declare it before God and others (cf. 1 Timothy 6:12, Romans 10:9–10).

Trusting in Jesus demands that we change our hearts and minds: to follow Jesus' original command to repent (Matthew 4:17, Acts 2:38). This means we make the decision to no longer live like we used to; we are committing ourselves to think, feel, and act like Jesus thought, felt, and acted. We then are to submit to immersion in water for remission of sin, dying to sin so that we can rise as new creatures, servants of Jesus (Acts 2:38, Romans 6:3–7, 1 Peter 3:21). It is at this point that we are considered disciples of Christ (Matthew 28:18–20). We are back in relationship with God.

But do you remember what Jesus said about that relationship in John 17:20–23?

> I do not ask for these only, but also for those who will believe in me through their word, that they may all be one, just as you, Father, are in me, and I in you, that they also may be in us, so that the world may believe that you have sent me. The glory that you have given me I have given to them, that they may be one even as we are one, I in them and you in me, that they may become perfectly one, so that the world may know that you sent me and loved them even as you loved me.

To truly be one, we must be "in" God the Son. Paul says in Romans 8:1–11 that the Spirit must be "in" us if we are going to be raised like Jesus was raised, and that this Spirit is the "Spirit of Christ." We are to "walk according" to that Spirit.

This discussion of God being "in" us and our being "in" God often gets confused because of our lack of understanding of the spiritual realm. But this much is clear: we are to be one with God in Christ as God the Father and God the Son are one. To be one like that is to be one in purpose and will.

This is why Paul declares the following in Galatians 2:20, 'I have been crucified with Christ. It is no longer I who live, but Christ who lives in me. And the life I now live in the flesh I live by faith in the Son of God, who loved me and gave himself for me.'

God has loved us; we ought to love God. To do that, we must "die" to ourselves so that we can "live" to Christ: we submit our will to God's, so that we can do what God would have us to do. But how can we know God's will?

We have been speaking about Jesus as the ONE Man, but we must never forget that He is God as well as Man. In fact, as John declares in John 1:18, Paul in Colossians 2:9, and the Hebrew author in Hebrews 1:3, Jesus maintains the fullness of God in bodily form, the exact imprint of the image of God. When we see the Son, we see the Father. In Jesus we have a demonstration of the love, mercy, grace, justice, kindness, patience, instruction, etc. of God. He truly is God the Word and God the Son, instructing us not just in word but also through His deeds.

Notice what Paul declares is our purpose in Romans 8:29, 'For those whom he foreknew he also predestined to be conformed to the image of his Son, in order that he might be the firstborn among many brothers.'

This makes sense. If we are going to have a restored relationship with God, we are going to have to become one with God as God is One within Himself. That can only happen when we begin to have the image of God as seen through Christ. This does not mean we become divine creatures or are elevated to godhood; we still fall short of God's glory (Romans 3:23). But it does mean that if we really do want a relationship with God, we are going to have to be a lot more like Jesus. If we want unity with God, we are going to have to learn how to think the way God would have us think, feel the way God would have us feel, and act the way God would have us act. This demands that we submit ourselves to God and follow His paths, not our own. We are going to have to commit to living righteously if we really want to be reconciled to God our Creator and to live in harmony with Him and the creation He made.

This will not happen overnight; it is a long and difficult process. We are not going to be able to do this on our own; it did not work that way before, and it is not going to work that way now. We will stumble often; the important thing is that we get up, ask for forgiveness, and maintain that trusting relationship with God. We can do all things through Christ who strengthens us (Philippians 4:13). God is willing to give us all things since He proved willing to give of His Son (Romans 8:31–32). God is willing and able to do far beyond what we can imagine if we only trust in Him (Ephesians 3:20–21).

God made us to enjoy relationship with Him. Our sins separated us from Him; in love, He reconciled us back to Him through the sacrifice of God the Son. We now can be restored in that relationship with God. But what does this have to do with others? We will consider this in ONE Another.

Questions for Discussion

1. What went wrong with the creation?

2. What are the consequences of sin?

3. What is justice? What does justice demand?

4. What can people do, on their own, to make up for their sin?

5. Who is the ONE Man? What did He do in life?

6. What did Jesus do that allowed us to be rescued from sin?

7. What did Jesus do that allowed us to be rescued from death?

8. What must be done to accept the reconciliation God offers?

9. How do we achieve unity with God as individuals?

ONE Another

'But if we walk in the light, as he is in the light, we have fellowship with one another, and the blood of Jesus his Son cleanses us from all sin' (1 John 1:7).

'But God has so composed the body, giving greater honor to the part that lacked it, that there may be no division in the body, but that the members may have the same care for one another' (1 Corinthians 12:24b–25).

WE HAVE SEEN THAT GOD is One in Three Persons, united in relationship, and He created man in His image to maintain relationship with Him. We have seen the problem of sin and mankind's inability to solve that problem on his own, and how sin has separated man from his God. Yet we have also learned that God loved mankind so much that He was willing to suffer the death of His Son so that we could be reconciled to Him and enjoy that relationship once more.

It is wonderful that we, as individuals, get to enjoy a relationship with God through Jesus Christ. But is that the only relationship after which we should seek? Is it all just about us as individuals standing before God? If that is the case, why do we still seek after relationships with our fellow man?

God's divine nature remains evident in His creation, particularly when it comes to man made in His image (Genesis 1:26–27, Romans 1:19–20). As God is relationally One, does it not make sense that we should seek relational unity with one another?

Jesus' Prayer for Believers

Let's return for a moment to the passage which we have frequently cited: John 17:20–23:

> I do not ask for these only, but also for those who will believe in me through their word, that they may all be one, just as you, Father, are in me, and I in you, that they also may be in us, so that the world may believe that you have sent me. The glory that you have given me I have given to them, that they may be one even as we are one, I in them and you in me, that they may become perfectly one, so that the world may know that you sent me and loved them even as you loved me.

Perhaps you have noticed that we have been addressing what this text explains to us without understanding it in context. John 17 presents the written record of a prayer Jesus offers before God in the Garden of Gethsemane the night He was betrayed. The first part of His prayer regards His twelve disciples who would soon be proclaiming the message of His Kingdom; they are the "these" spoken of in John 17:20 (cf. John 17:1–19).

Please notice that Jesus begins to speak about "those who will believe in [Him] through [the apostles'] word" in John 17:20. Who are those people? They certainly include all of the Christians in the first century who heard the message of the Gospel directly from the apostles.

But have we not also believed in Jesus through the message of the apostles as it is revealed in the New Testament?

If so, does not Jesus' message relate to us?

What does Jesus pray for regarding all those who will believe in Him through the apostles' message?

That they may all be one!

Believers in Christ, therefore, are to be one just as God the Father, God the Son, and God the Holy Spirit are one. That is the contextual message of John 17:20-23. We have seen how God is One in relational unity; we have seen how we can be reconciled to God through the blood of Jesus His Son; now we must understand that God wants us to be one, not just with Him, but also with one another!

The Body of Christ

How is it that we are to be one with God and yet also one with each other? Paul attempts to explain this to us in Romans 12:4-5, 'For as in one body we have many members, and the members do not all have the same function, so we, though many, are one body in Christ, and individually members one of another.'

Paul uses the image of God's people as the body of Christ. He does not at all mean that God's people are physically Christ's body: he knows that Jesus was raised in the flesh and ascended to Heaven (cf. 1 Corinthians 15). He is stressing that the relationships between God's people are important, just like the relationship between the believer and God.

We understand in a physical body there are many different parts that have individual functions. Nevertheless, the different parts with their individual functions work together as one entity. As it is in a physical body, so it is among God's people. Each person is a member of the body of Christ. Each person is connected in relationship to God. By virtue of the shared connection they have with God, they are connected to one another!

This image helps us to understand many things about how God's people are to be one with each other. Paul declares that Christ is the head of His body in Colossians 1:18: just as all human body parts act independently and with each other at the direction of the head, so it is in the body of Christ. Everyone follows the commands of Jesus; that is the basis of how we relate to God and to one another. Likewise, as both Romans 12:3-8 and 1 Corinthians 12:12-27 explain, just as the human body has different parts that perform different functions, some more public and obvious, others more private and discreet, and yet all are necessary for proper functioning, so it is in the body of Christ. Individual people come with different abilities, talents, and experiences, and yet each can use those abilities and talents to serve God and each other, some more publicly and obviously, others more privately and discreetly, and all such people are necessary for the body of Christ to function the way God wants.

The very idea of one body is quite radical, as Paul makes clear:

> There is neither Jew nor Greek, there is neither slave nor free, there is no male and female, for you are all one in Christ Jesus. (Galatians 3:28)

> Here there is not Greek and Jew, circumcised and uncircumcised, barbarian, Scythian, slave, free; but Christ is all, and in all. (Colossians 3:11)

We know all too well that people find all kinds of ways to build barriers against one another. People are often divided on account of age, ethnicity, language, race, culture, class, politics, geography: even sports teams! Some of these are serious barriers. But consider what Paul says in Ephesians 2:13–16:

> But now in Christ Jesus you who once were far off have been brought near by the blood of Christ. For he himself is our peace, who has made us both one and has broken down in his flesh the dividing wall of hostility by abolishing the law of commandments expressed in ordinances, that he might create in himself one new man in place of the two, so making peace, and might reconcile us both to God in one body through the cross, thereby killing the hostility.

In context, Paul is saying that on the cross Jesus set aside the Law of

Moses that served as the barrier of unity between Jews and Gentiles. In so doing, He kills the source of hostility between the Jews and the Gentiles, allowing the two to become one, making peace, reconciling all to God in one body.

What Paul says regarding Jews and Gentiles stands true for any other thing that would divide people from each other. The color of our skin, the language we speak, how much money we make, where we come from, whatever political views we may hold: all these things that divide people are overcome through the love of God in Christ Jesus.

The unity of being God's people in Christ should be far stronger than anything the world might use to try to divide us!

God's Eternal Purpose

So, God's people must be one with each other just as they are one with God. What is the form that this body takes?

"And [Christ] is the head of the body, the church. He is the beginning, the firstborn from the dead, that in everything he might be preeminent" (Colossians 1:18).

Paul identifies the *church* as the body of Christ here in Colossians 1:18. While this emphasis on the church may seem surprising to some, the New Testament constantly speaks of how God's people work together as the church. God's eternal purpose is manifest in the church, as Paul declares in Ephesians 3:10–11, "So that through the church the manifold wisdom of God might now be made known to the rulers and authorities in the heavenly places. This was according to the eternal purpose that he has realized in Christ Jesus our YHWH."

What is that "manifold wisdom" of God? That all men who believe in God and serve Him—Jew and Gentile, no matter what race, gender, class, and so forth—have a share in Christ, are members of the same body, and partake of the promise in Christ through the Gospel (Ephesians 3:6).

The image of the body is one image that describes how God intends for the church to function. Another image is that of a family: fellow believers are like brothers and sisters, with God as Father and Jesus as their elder brother (Romans 8:15-17, Hebrews 2:10-12, 17). Still another is that of a temple: Jesus the chief cornerstone, the apostles and prophets the foundation, and believers joined together upon it as living stones (Ephesians 2:19-22, 1 Peter 2:4-8).

All these pictures are designed to show us what the church is supposed to be: a group of people who love each other, care for each other, and try to strengthen one another. While all people who believe in God and serve Him are part of the church, the universal group of believers, smaller, more local groups meet as local churches (like the church in Corinth, 1 Corinthians 1:2, or the church in Thessalonica, 1 Thessalonians 1:1). The local church, shepherded by qualified men who serve as elders whenever possible (cf. 1 Timothy 3:1-8, 1 Peter 5:1-4), comes together to strengthen and encourage its members through remembering the death of Jesus in YHWH's Supper, singing hymns together, praying together, hearing God's word preached together, giving together, and reading the Bible together (Acts 20:7, 1 Corinthians 10:16-17, 11:23-26, 14:15-17, 14:26, 16:1-3, Ephesians 5:19, 1 Timothy 4:13, Hebrews 10:25). They also spend time together in one another's homes (1 Peter 4:9), getting to know one another, enjoying one another's company in many different settings.

Paul summarizes how the church is supposed to work most beautifully in Ephesians 4:11-16:

> And he gave the apostles, the prophets, the evangelists, the shepherds and teachers, to equip the saints for the work of ministry, for building up the body of Christ, until we all

attain to the unity of the faith and of the knowledge of the Son of God, to mature manhood, to the measure of the stature of the fullness of Christ, so that we may no longer be children, tossed to and fro by the waves and carried about by every wind of doctrine, by human cunning, by craftiness in deceitful schemes. Rather, speaking the truth in love, we are to grow up in every way into him who is the head, into Christ, from whom the whole body, joined and held together by every joint with which it is equipped, when each part is working properly, makes the body grow so that it builds itself up in love.

The Bible reveals that the church is supposed to be a group of people dedicated to growing and strengthening themselves, each other, and everyone who might draw near. This stands in stark contrast with the way that a lot of religious organizations function, and the way that a lot of people think about the church. Many times, people think of the church as a building, or a large religious organization, or just in terms of its assemblies. The church was never a building or a highly structured religious organization in the New Testament; while the church does assemble, the church is intended to be much more than just its Sunday meetings. God wants to see people grow and be strengthened in their relationships with one another just as He wants people to grow and be strengthened in their relationship with Him.

How to Be One

We have seen that God's people are to be one. We have seen that God's people are identified as the church, and the church can be understood in terms of a human body, or a family. But how are we to become one? This is precisely what Jesus is addressing in John 17:20–23 (emphasis mine):

> I do not ask for these only, but also for **those who will believe in me through their word, that they may all be**

one, just as you, Father, are in me, and I in you, that they also may be in us, so that the world may believe that you have sent me. The glory that you have given me I have given to them, **that they may be one even as we are one, I in them and you in me, that they may become perfectly one**, so that the world may know that you sent me and loved them even as you loved me.

The unity of God's people is to reflect the unity that exists within God Himself. As we noted in ONE God, God is One in nature, character, mind, purpose/will and thus One in love and relationship (Matthew 26:39, John 1:1, 14:6–11, 1 John 4:7–21).

Therefore, if we will be perfectly one, we will seek unity in nature, character, purpose/will, and thus in love and relationship!

The rest of the New Testament confirms this. As we have already seen, all of us can be one in Christ as fellow human beings, with no one of greater value than any other because of social standing, class, culture, and the like (Galatians 3:28, Colossians 3:11). Paul says that all should seek to be conformed to the image of the Son (Romans 8:29). This is easily seen in the contrast between the works of the flesh and the fruit of the Spirit in Galatians 5:17–24. All believers are to avoid the works of the flesh and to exhibit the fruit of the Spirit, not just some! Paul declares in 1 Corinthians 1:10 that believers are to be united in the same mind and the same judgment, living in agreement, not division.

Yet everything comes together with the idea of love as seeking the best interest of the beloved; little wonder then, that Jesus declares the following in John 13:35, "By this all people will know that you are my disciples, if you have love for one another."

Unity is not easy; it does not come without effort. Think about what God had to do to reconcile us to Him! We must put effort into developing and maintaining unity. Perhaps the greatest exhortation

to unity can be found in Philippians 2:1–4:
> So if there is any encouragement in Christ, any comfort from love, any participation in the Spirit, any affection and sympathy, complete my joy by being of the same mind, having the same love, being in full accord and of one mind. Do nothing from rivalry or conceit, but in humility count others more significant than yourselves. Let each of you look not only to his own interests, but also to the interests of others.

As God is and has acted within Himself, so we are to act with each other. God is love within Himself and toward His creation; thus, we are to love one another (1 John 4:7–21). God is in agreement with Himself; so we are to be in agreement with one another (1 Corinthians 1:10). The Son proved willing to humble Himself to accomplish God's will; so we must humble ourselves in general and toward one another to accomplish God's will (Philippians 2:5–11, 1 Peter 5:5). As God has served within Himself and for us, so we are to serve God and one another (Matthew 20:25–28, 1 Peter 4:10). As God shows great care within Himself and for us, so we are to care for one another and bear one another's burdens (Galatians 6:2). We could provide many more examples since the New Testament is full of commands and exhortations about how we are to treat one another. This goes to show just how important it is for us to seek unity with one another as we seek to be one with God!

This connects with the other images the New Testament has provided. In a family, there must be some attempt toward agreement on ideas and behavior for the family to be unified. That family must also work to build relationships among its members if there will be any lasting connection, and that requires people to work with each other. The same is true with a body; what would happen to a body if different parts wanted to go in different ways or refused to work with each other? What if some parts of the body thought that they were better than other parts of the body? Things would not go well! What kind of Temple would exist if some blocks were in one location, and other blocks were far away from them, without connection among them? A family, a body, a temple: for these to be understood as one, the different parts must be joined together with deep connections in agreement. Anything less is not real unity!

One Another

Unity is never easy; as humans who still fall short of God's glory, we are not going to realize that unity perfectly on our own (Romans 3:23). But this is not an excuse for us to not aspire to the goal of unity.

Our unity with one another is nicely expressed in 1 John 1:7, "But if we walk in the light, as he is in the light, we have fellowship with one another, and the blood of Jesus his Son cleanses us from all sin."

Unity must start with walking in the light of God. We must be seeking that relationship with God, no longer thinking, feeling, and acting like we used to in our sinful lives, but trying to think, feel, and act like Jesus.

As we seek to live like Jesus, we will notice other people who are also seeking to live like Jesus. We will notice them because we are all on the same path of Christ (Matthew 7:13–14). We have that relationship with each other not because of anything special about us; that relationship exists because we individually have relationships with God in Christ. Since we are thus reckoned as members of His body (cf. Romans 12:3–7), we are to forge connections with one another.

When we walk in the light and associate with one another, the blood of Christ will cleanse us from sin. We maintain our relationship with God, and, we are to have relationships with one another.

The challenges are great, but the rewards are far greater. There are some people with whom it is hard to get along; sometimes the differences that exist among people seem hard to overcome. But when we find unity, we find ourselves at home and at rest. When we find oneness with God and with one another, we obtain life in community for which we have yearned. We do not have to be alone. We do not have to think that we are going to trudge through life without traveling companions. We can have a relationship with God. Through that relationship with God, we can have fellowship with one another and encourage one another on the journey we call life.

It is the way God always intended it to be.

We have learned about ONE God, ONE Man, and ONE Another. In the next lesson we will put it all together in the ONE Story.

Questions for Discussion

1. Whom is Jesus praying for in John 17:20–23, and for what reason?

2. What does it mean for God's people to be the "body of Christ"?

3. Why is the church so important in the New Testament?

4. How is the church supposed to function?

5. How do we seek true unity? Who is our model, and how?

6. On what basis can we have true relationship with God and with one another?

ONE Story

And all these, though commended through their faith, did not receive what was promised, since God had provided something better for us, that apart from us they should not be made perfect. Therefore, since we are surrounded by so great a cloud of witnesses, let us also lay aside every weight, and sin which clings so closely, and let us run with endurance the race that is set before us, looking to Jesus, the founder and perfecter of our faith, who for the joy that was set before him endured the cross, despising the shame, and is seated at the right hand of the throne of God (Hebrews 11:39–12:2).

We have covered a lot of ground together. We have learned about the ONE God, how God is one in relational unity, and how He in love created the universe and humans so that we might be able to share in relationship with Him. We have seen the problem of sin and how it separated us from God, and how God loved us enough to send the ONE Man to teach us how to live like Him, to die so that we could receive forgiveness of sin and rise again to give us hope for eternal life. We have discovered that in Christ we can establish true relationships with ONE Another and establish the type of unity for which Jesus prayed in John 17:20–23.

Even though we have covered a lot of ground together, we can look at the Bible and see that there are plenty of things we have barely mentioned. Does everything we have learned so far "fit" the rest of Scripture?

As we finish this study together, let us look at the ONE Story and see if what we have learned fits in with everything taught in Scripture. As we do, we might be surprised to see how God has been seeking to restore mankind through relationships He established throughout time, and that we ourselves have our own role to play in the story as well!

In the Beginning
Bible passages: Genesis 1–2

The ONE Story is really an eternal story, for its Author is eternal (Ephesians 3:10–11). God the Father, God the Son, and God the Holy Spirit have always been, are, and always will be One God in Three Persons, relationally one in love (cf. Revelation 4:8).

But for our purposes, the story begins with the creation of the universe and all that is in it, described in Genesis 1 and 2. God spoke the creation into existence by His Word. Everything had its place. Mankind was created in God's image to work the ground and to be the steward of the creation. The first man and woman, Adam and Eve, were placed in the Garden of Eden. They enjoyed a face-to-face relationship with God their Creator and were innocent of sin, evil, and death. God's creation was deemed "very good" (Genesis 1:31); God was satisfied.

Man's Fall
Bible passages: Genesis 3–11
(for explanations, see Romans 1:18–26, 5:12–18, 8:19–23).

Adam and Eve were not robots; God did not force or compel them to do what He wanted them to do. He gave one commandment to them: they were not to eat the fruit of the tree of the knowledge of good and evil (Genesis 2:17). The serpent in the Garden, later identified as Satan (cf. Revelation 12:9), tempted Eve with the fruit of that tree. He challenged Eve's view of why God made such a commandment and suggested that God was simply trying to keep Eve from being like Him (Genesis 3:4–5). Eve was tempted by the fruit's appearance, its ability to satisfy hunger, and the wisdom it would bring, so she ate of it and persuaded Adam to eat as well (Genesis 3:6–7).

The consequences were immediate and severe. Yes, Adam and Eve now knew good and evil, and they were ashamed of their naked appearance. They had disobeyed God and thus had rebelled against their Creator; consequently, they suffered separation from God, physically and spiritually. They would soon no longer enjoy a face-to-face relationship with God; they were cast out of the Garden and compelled to work the land for food (Genesis 3:8–24). While they did not physically die that day, they began dying that day: by their deed, sin and death had entered the world, and the whole creation was now subject to corruption and decay (Romans 5:12–19, 8:19–23). All sorts of miseries, including pain, suffering, sickness, violence, and death, became reality in God's creation. They now had a very real sin problem: they had transgressed God's command, and the penalty they suffered for it was death.

Man's fall did not end with Adam and Eve. We begin seeing terrible sin in the very next generation: Adam and Eve's son, Cain, kills their other son Abel (Genesis 4:1–8). Human sin and propensity to sin increased to the point that within ten generations of Adam and Eve, we are told that the "wickedness of man was great in the earth, and that every intention of the thoughts of his heart was only evil continually" (Genesis 6:5). This complete depravity merited a drastic action: God brings a flood upon the whole world and all perish except Noah, a man who found favor in God's sight, his family, and the animals with him on the ark (Genesis 6–9).

While people experienced separation from God, they still maintained unity amongst themselves, until about five generations after Noah and the Flood. All the people of the world at that time met at Shinar and began building a tower there to make a name for themselves so that they would not be scattered. Since man was using his unity toward such selfish ends, God confused their language and they ultimately scattered across the whole earth; the tower would be known as the Tower of Babel, where Babylon would be built (Genesis 11:1–9).

Man's fall was as complete as it was thorough. He found himself separated from God, separated from one another, without hope, without a state, without commitment with each other and with God, and without redemption. Humans scattered everywhere; while they understood they were missing something and not complete in and of themselves, in their rebellion against God, they did not give Him honor but made gods out of the natural forces He set in motion. In such environments sin increased, and so did the distance between God and man. That divide was not going to be bridged by humans as they fumbled in darkness (cf. Romans 1:18–26).

God Begins Restoring the Relationship
Bible passages: Genesis 12–50

Not long after man reached the depth of sinfulness and separation from God, we are told God calls one man out of service to false gods to believe in Him and follow Him. This man was called Abram, later re-named Abraham. God told Abraham to leave the center of civilization at that time, Ur, and to go to a mostly rural area known as Canaan (Genesis 12:1–9). God promised to bless Abram if he followed Him; Abraham believed in God, trusted in God, and maintained a relationship with God. God promised Abraham that he would have a son with Sarah his wife, and that his descendants through that son would inherit the land of Canaan. That son would be known as Isaac, and after Abraham proved willing to offer Isaac back up to God, God promised that through Abraham's seed all the nations of the earth would be blessed (Genesis 22:18; cf. Genesis 12–24). We will soon see how these promises were fulfilled; nevertheless, we can see here that God ultimately intends to reconcile all men to Himself through the relationship He is developing with Abraham and his descendants.

Isaac will have a son named Jacob who will inherit the promise. In a critical moment in the development of Jacob's faith in God, Jacob finds himself wrestling with an angel. After wrestling all night, the angel blesses Jacob with a new name: Israel, which means "wrestles with God." This Jacob will have twelve sons by four women, and the promise of Abraham would extend to the descendants of all twelve.

God and Israel
Bible Passages: Exodus 1—Malachi 4

God now wanted to work with a whole nation, not just a series of individuals. Important work had to be done: this nation had to learn that they needed to depend on God and trust Him alone, as Abraham, Isaac, and Jacob had to learn. They had to understand there is only one God, and He has power, and the false gods of the nations do not.

These lessons had to be learned the hard way. All of Jacob's descendants found themselves in Egypt on account of a famine in the days of Jacob; after some time, these Israelites were enslaved by the Egyptian rulers. They were forced to endure hard service at the hands of the most powerful nation of the day who trusted in all sorts of gods. God chose one man, Moses, to lead Israel out of Egypt so that He could fulfill the promises He made to Israel's ancestors. God brought all sorts of plagues upon the Egyptians, ultimately devastating their river, their crops, their livestock, their firstborn children, and even their army (Exodus 1–14). Soon the Israelites had crossed the Red Sea as free people. God had rescued them from slavery. He had proven to Israel and ultimately to all the surrounding nations that He was God with great power.

God then led the Israelites deep into the desert wilderness of the Sinai Peninsula and modern-day northwest Saudi Arabia (Exodus 15–Deuteronomy 34). Israel depended on God for food, drink, and protection. At Mount Sinai God spoke directly to the Israelites, declaring that He wanted to be the God of Israel and that Israel would be His people (Exodus 19:4–6). He wanted to enter into a covenant, an agreement or commitment, with Israel: He would be their God, would give them the good land of Canaan in which they could live, and He would bless them, as long as they trusted in Him alone as God and followed His instructions which He provided. The Israelites agreed to this covenant.

God then spent a lot of time providing to Israel laws and guidelines. Some of the laws dealt with things the Israelites should or should not do; these are encapsulated in the Ten Commandments in Exodus 20:1–17. Many of the laws dealt with sacrifices: the Israelites had to learn about how sin is covered, or atoned, by sacrificing innocent animals to cover for their sins, and to offer other sacrifices to keep peace with God and to honor Him with the best of their produce. Other laws dealt with the location for these sacrifices, known as the Tabernacle, and its construction; festivals and guidelines about purity and holiness were also established. God also established that the Levites, one of the tribes of Israel, would serve Him as priests, responsible for making these sacrifices and teaching the people God's instructions (Leviticus 1–27).

All these instructions were very important: they were a guide to understand, in a very physical way, what was necessary to maintain a spiritual relationship with God. Humans, deeply lost in their sinfulness in their turning away from God, needed this instruction with its very physical ideas of sacrifice, holiness, and purity, if humans would ever be able to fully appreciate the more spiritual instruction that would come later.

God intended for all the Israelites to serve Him as priests, having fully conquered the land of Canaan, and He would be their King and Leader. But just as sin complicated God's original intentions for mankind, Israel's sins complicated God's intentions for them. While still at Mount Sinai, the Israelites created a god for themselves out of gold; when Moses confronts them, only the Levites stood on God's side (Exodus 32:1–26). From that point on only the Levites could serve directly before God.

Israel persisted in sin. Complaining to God; at every point when their faith was tested in the desert wilderness, they sinned. That generation was cursed to die in the desert wilderness because of their faithlessness. The next generation, led by Joshua, would enter the land of Canaan, and would possess much of the hill country.

But even they did not faithfully execute God's command: much of the land was left unconquered (Numbers–Joshua).

God had fulfilled many of His promises to Abraham. Abraham's descendants, the Israelites, were His people, despite their many sins. They lived in the land of Canaan, now known as Israel. But all was not well.

Even though God had explicitly warned the Israelites not to adopt the customs of the Canaanites around them, soon after taking over the land, the Israelites began to build statues and altars to the false gods of the Canaanites. As punishment, God would allow a foreign nation to control parts of Israel; when the Israelites would change their ways, He would select a person, known as a judge, who would deliver Israel from the oppressor. This happened time and time again, and things only got worse. The judges themselves: and especially their children, were not as noble as those who came before them. After awhile the people had enough: they wanted a king like all the other nations (Judges–1 Samuel 8).

Israel had rebelled against God yet again. But God allowed them to have their king. The first king, Saul, was chosen because of his stature; his character did not prove to be so wonderful. It was the second king anointed at God's command, named David, who trusted in God and would fully deliver God's people. By God's help, David defeated Israel's enemies and brought peace and security to the land. David would establish Jerusalem as his capital city; his son Solomon would build a temple for God there, (1 Samuel 8–1 Kings 10; 1 Chronicles 10–2 Chronicles 10).

Kings proved to be Israel's final undoing. After Solomon the kingdom was divided, with David's descendant ruling in Judah to the south, and other rulers in Israel to the north. Jeroboam, the first king of Israel in the north, built two temples and placed bull statues in them; all kings after him would follow in that idolatry. Some kings of Judah followed God; others did not.

It was during these days that the prophets began to actively work among Israel. Prophets were people whom God entrusted with a message for Israel and Judah. Elijah was the most famous prophet; he stood up against the service to the idol Baal in Israel. We know much about what the prophets said because we have many of their writings. They consistently commanded, exhorted, and begged the Israelites to stop serving other gods and return to God and serve Him only. They consistently described Israel's service to other gods as adultery, and God was the "husband" who could only tolerate so much of His "wife's" infidelity. The prophets warned Israel that if they did not stop following other gods, God would prove yet again that He was the only God. This time, however, Israel would suffer the punishment (1 Kings 17–2 Kings 36; Isaiah–Malachi).

While some people listened to the prophets, most did not. The consequences of which the prophets warned came to pass. The northern Kingdom of Israel was overrun by the Assyrians and its population completely exiled, most of whom would never return. A few generations later the Kingdom of Judah was overrun by the Babylonians. God's temple in Jerusalem was destroyed and most of the people exiled to Babylon, just as the prophets warned.

When the Persians began to rule after the Babylonians, many of the inhabitants of Judah, now often called Jews, returned to the land of Israel. Over time they rebuilt Jerusalem and its temple, although it was not as glorious as it was in previous days. The Jews who returned had mostly learned their lesson; they believed in God alone and tried to trust in Him (Ezra–Nehemiah).

But they were not totally free people. The Persians, followed by the Greeks, and then the Romans ruled over their land. Yet the Israelites cherished a hope that they were given by their prophets. While the prophets warned about the punishment Israel would receive, they also spoke about how God would restore their fortunes afterward. The prophets spoke about One from the line of David who would be given power and authority. They spoke of One who would suffer the consequences of the sins of the people upon Himself. He would triumph over all the nations, and all nations would learn of God through Him. It would be upon this Man that Israel set their hope.

Emmanuel, God With Us
Bible passages: Matthew 1—John 21

Around two thousand years ago the time was right. The fourth empire predicted by Daniel was ruling: the Romans had conquered the entire Mediterranean Sea basin. Travel had never been easier and would not be again for 1,900 years; overall the entire area was at peace; most of the people understood the same language, Greek. The temple in Jerusalem was being rebuilt in a magnificent way by Herod the Great, and the Jewish people were tired of the oppression of Herod and the Romans. The Spirit had been silent for about 400 years, and then, just before Herod died, the angel Gabriel visited a priest named Zechariah and a teenage girl named Mary and her carpenter husband–to–be, Joseph. Zechariah, in his old age, would have a son named John who would prepare the way for YHWH; Mary would conceive a child by the Holy Spirit who would be that YHWH.

The conditions were exactly as the prophets had said. The fourth empire was ruling; there was the one who would prepare the way of YHWH; the Child was born of a virgin, in Bethlehem, to a descendant of David. But it certainly was not happening in the way that most of the Jewish people had expected. He was not raised in Jerusalem but in Nazareth of Galilee, an insignificant village in an outlying portion of Israel. He was not born in luxury or power but into a family of peasants. He was not formally educated.

This was the pattern for the life of Jesus of Nazareth. He was saying and doing the things that the prophets of old had said that their Deliverer – their King, the Anointed One (in Hebrew, the Messiah; in Greek, the Christ) – would say and do. But He was not saying it and doing it in the way the Jewish people had come to expect.

During Jesus' baptism in the Jordan River by John the Baptist, the one who prepared the way before Him, the Father and the Spirit bore witness that the Triune God was working through Jesus. Jesus suffered temptation in the desert at the hands of Satan; whereas Adam sinned when tempted, Jesus did not. For three years Jesus traveled around the historical region of Israel: Galilee, Samaria, the Decapolis, and Judea. While many followed Him, He chose twelve men – mostly uneducated fishermen and other laborers, a tax collector, and a revolutionary or two – to form a select band of disciples to whom He provided greater instruction. He performed many powerful signs that demonstrated the power of God rested in Him. He taught the people with authority, not like the religious leaders in whom the people had put their trust. He acted and spoke in ways that reminded the people of Moses, Elijah, and other holy men of old. He commanded people to change their ways and prepare for the Kingdom of God that He said was coming very soon.

People knew there was something different about Jesus of Nazareth. He made extraordinary claims: He claimed to be the Son of God, that He and the Father were one, and identified Himself with the very name of God: YHWH. These claims were not disproven. The religious authorities could not stand Jesus, but they could not withstand His arguments, either.

During the Jewish festival of Passover, the annual reminder of God's deliverance of Israel from the Egyptians, Jesus entered Jerusalem in triumph. His disciples, His followers, and the whole city was expecting Him to set up His Kingdom there and begin ruling; they imagined that He would start by clearing out the Romans. Instead, He cleared out the temple. He challenged the religious authorities. Ultimately, He was betrayed by one of His disciples, and the same crowds that hailed Him a week earlier now cried out for His execution. He was beaten and then hung to die on a cross by crucifixion, one of the most humiliating and painful ways that one can be killed. Thus, Jesus of Nazareth died, executed like a political insurrectionist.

Jesus' disciples and followers were despondent and confused. How could this have happened? But then, on the third day after His crucifixion, some of His female followers came to His tomb and found it empty. Jesus then appeared to the women, and then His disciples and followers, as resurrected from the dead, just as He had said during His lifetime. He explained to them what had happened.

While the Jewish people were looking for deliverance from the Romans, God wanted to deliver everyone from the greater enemy: Satan, sin, and death. As the sacrificial system had taught the Israelites, there had to be a penalty paid for sin; Jesus, who had not sinned in life, could be the ultimate sacrifice for sin. As the one man Adam had sinned and sin thus spread throughout humanity and increased, so the "new Adam," Jesus, by one act of sacrifice could atone, or cover all the sins that had spread throughout humanity. All the evil that plagued mankind Jesus experienced in His sufferings and death; by rising from the dead, He gained the victory over sin, sickness, and death. Through His resurrection people could have hope for life after death: as God raised Him from the dead with power, so on the final day He would raise everyone from the dead!

Jesus explained how all the messages of the Old Testament were fulfilled in Him. He had a priestly function in His death, like a priesthood that existed long before Levi and their priesthood. He was the suffering Servant spoken of by Isaiah. In fact, throughout His life, Jesus was the embodiment of the story of Israel: just as Israel left the land for Egypt, then came out of Egypt during the Exodus, dwelt in the land, was exiled, and returned, so Jesus had to go to Egypt as a boy, came back to the land of Israel, lived, died (exile), and was raised again in power (returned).

Yet, Jesus was more than just the story of Israel: He was God the Word, God the Son, made flesh. He was the Emmanuel, literally translated, "God with us." He was sent by the Father in love to reconcile mankind back to God: by taking on flesh, showing mankind how to live by His example and teaching, Jesus becomes the bridge that spans the wide separation between God and man. Jesus was able to undo what Adam had done; Jesus also pointed the way to the "new creation" in the resurrection.

The Kingdom
Bible passages: Acts 1—Revelation 22

Jesus lived, died, and was raised again in power. Forty days after His resurrection, He ascended back to heaven where God the Father gave Him all power and authority. Jesus was now ruling over the Kingdom concerning which He had spoken so much in His lifetime! This Kingdom was not going to be a physical Kingdom with a human king sitting on a throne somewhere; God's rule in Christ was over people who lived under all kinds of different earthly rulers. Whereas earthly kingdoms have come and gone, God's Kingdom—the people who trust in Him and follow His ways – still continues!

Ten days after Jesus' ascension, or fifty days after His resurrection, many Jewish people from three continents returned to Jerusalem for Pentecost, the memorial of when God declared the Ten Commandments to Israel from Mount Sinai. Suddenly, the Holy Spirit fell upon the band of disciples, now known as apostles, whom Jesus instructed more deeply. They began speaking in different foreign languages which they did not know but the people hearing them did. The people were hearing all about the deeds of God in their own language! One of the twelve, Simon Peter, addressed the crowd by declaring God had raised Jesus from the dead, of which they were witnesses, and that in so doing God declared Jesus, YHWH and Christ. Over three thousand of the Jewish people assembled that day believed Peter's message, changed their hearts and minds, and were baptized, or immersed in water, in the name of Jesus for the forgiveness of their sins. The church: the manifestation of Jesus' Kingdom on earth: had begun (Acts 2).

The Holy Spirit's action on the day of Pentecost is very significant in its meaning. There is a reason why His power was made evident through speaking in different languages. It was at the Tower of Babel when God confused man's language, and that was the point at which man first was separated from his fellow man. The Holy Spirit, by communicating God's one message in many different languages at once, was declaring that in Christ and His Kingdom, not only was man no longer separated from his God, but he would no longer need to be separated from his fellow man.

The prophets had declared that through Jesus the other nations of the world, called "Gentiles" by the Jewish people, would come to the knowledge of the God of Israel, the One True God. Therefore, not long after the message that Jesus was YHWH had spread throughout Judea, Samaria, and Galilee, God sends a powerful sign to Simon Peter. Peter is summoned to tell the good news about Jesus to a Roman soldier named Cornelius, even though he was not a Jewish person. While Peter preached the message of Jesus to him, the Holy Spirit fell upon Cornelius and the other Gentiles around him, just as it had fallen upon Peter and the apostles on Pentecost (Acts 10). God was reconciling Himself to all men through Jesus, not just Israelites!

Within forty years of Jesus' death and resurrection, the good news of Jesus and His Kingdom, called the Gospel, had spread even to Rome itself. The apostles, along with a convert named Paul, and many other Christians, had told thousands of people about who Jesus was and what He had done for mankind. Small groups of believers had formed in many cities in Italy, Greece, Turkey, Israel, and Egypt.

Throughout his work in preaching the Gospel, Paul had established new groups of believers, organized into local churches, mostly in Turkey and Greece. He kept up correspondence with them even when he was away or imprisoned. Many of the letters he sent were kept, for the Holy Spirit had inspired their contents, and they were useful not just for the churches to whom they were sent, but for believers throughout time, to understand the message of the good news of Jesus Christ.

Likewise, the apostles Matthew and John, along with Mark the associate of Peter and Luke the associate of Paul, wrote the story of Jesus' life in what we call the four Gospels so that people throughout time could know what Jesus had said and done. The same apostles Peter and John also wrote letters, as did James and Jude the half–brothers of Jesus. All of these would come together to form the New Testament, the record of what Jesus and the apostles said, did, and taught.

In these letters, the apostles work out just how Christians are to believe and work with each other. They make it clear how Jesus and His Kingdom fit well within the ONE Story. We have seen how Jesus was the "new Adam," undoing what the "first Adam" had done. We have seen how God seeks to reconcile man through Christ, evidenced in the speaking in tongues on the day of Pentecost and by Cornelius and his men, undoing the separation that happened at the Tower of Babel. Paul goes on to show how God's promise to Abraham that the descendant through whom all the nations of the earth would be blessed was Jesus Himself, and that everyone who trusts in God like Abraham did is the spiritual inheritor of the promise and thus the spiritual descendant of Abraham (Galatians 3).

We have seen how Jesus embodied the story of Israel; the apostles demonstrated that what God taught to the world through Israel in a physical and shadowy way, He was now demonstrating to the world through Jesus' kingdom, the church, in a spiritual and real way. Israel was a physical nation whom God redeemed from slavery and set apart; the church represents people from different physical nations who are made into one spiritual kingdom; in Christ, God redeemed them, and they are spiritually set apart. Israel had a very physical idea of holiness involving cleanliness laws and sacrifices; in Jesus, God demonstrated true holiness, and His people in the church are to offer themselves as spiritual sacrifices. In Israel, God's presence dwelt in a physical temple; in the church, God dwells spiritually with all in His kingdom, individually and collectively. The apostles demonstrated that God's work in building a relationship with Israel was to provide a means of understanding what He was going to do in building a relationship with anyone who would return to Him through Jesus the Christ. God's covenant, or commitment, with Israel was a physical shadow of the real spiritual covenant God would make with all men in Jesus.

Sadly, even though they should have been the first to understand and accept Jesus, and to share in that new covenant, many Jewish people had rejected Him, both during His life and after His resurrection. Around forty years after Jesus' death and resurrection, they tried to take matters into their own hands and rebelled against the Romans. The Romans came, defeated them, destroyed their city and their temple, just as the prophets and Jesus had predicted. It has not been restored since. The sign is there for those who seek to understand.

By the end of the first century CE, the apostles had died, and with them, new revelations about what God had accomplished in Jesus. What had been recorded in the New Testament was enough for people throughout time to know who God is, what He has done, especially through Jesus, and how man can be reconciled to God and become like Jesus. We can still hear the words of Jesus and the apostles today in its pages!

The final message God communicated through the apostles was given to John, and it is known as Revelation. In Revelation, many of the themes that have been present throughout the Bible come back vividly, describing how God will be victorious over the spiritual forces of darkness and the Roman power through whom those forces of darkness work. We are given a glimpse there of the majesty of God enthroned and the glory which God seeks to give to all those who trust in Jesus and have been obedient to Him. The final scenes of Revelation describes the final day of this world, a message described often in the preaching and teaching of the apostles. On that day, Jesus will return to earth and take on the role God gave Him as Judge of all mankind. Those who did not seek a relationship with God or proved unwilling to do the will of God the Father, will find themselves separated from God for all eternity. Those who sought relationship with God through Him and who did the will of God the Father will share in the resurrection of eternal life. In that scene, the kingdom, God's people, are pictured as glorified beyond measure, dwelling in some type of new heaven and earth, with God in their midst, in a scene reminiscent of the Garden of Eden. The end of the telling of the ONE Story, therefore, is as its beginning: God and man having a face-to-face relationship, unbroken, but this time having conquered pain, sin, and death through Jesus in the resurrection. We will understand fully. We will know as we are known. We will be fully satisfied through God our Creator.

Your Role in the ONE Story

It is true that everything we have just described happened and was written down thousands of years ago. Yet God's plan is an eternal plan (Ephesians 3:10–11); God is still sustaining the creation (Hebrews 1:3); therefore, we can trust that God is active today and is as interested in us as He was interested in all of those people long ago.

We can look back to all the characters of the Bible—Adam, Noah, Abraham, Jacob, Moses, David, and so on and so forth—and we may find their examples to be wonderful. But it is easy to feel that we are not like they were. They heard directly from God; they seemed to have more faith than we do. They knew their role in God's story.

But let us again return to what the Hebrew author wrote in Hebrews 11:39–12:2:

> And all these, though commended through their faith, did not receive what was promised, since God had provided something better for us, that apart from us they should not be made perfect. Therefore, since we are surrounded by so great a cloud of witnesses, let us also lay aside every weight, and sin which clings so closely, and let us run with endurance the race that is set before us, looking to Jesus, the founder and perfecter of our faith, who for the joy that was set before him endured the cross, despising the shame, and is seated at the right hand of the throne of God.

What does he mean that they did not receive what was promised? What does it mean that apart from us they should not be made perfect?

The Hebrew author is telling both his audience and us that we have our part to play in the ONE Story as well. We believe that God is still rescuing people from sin, darkness, and death through Jesus.

We believe that God still seeks for people to enjoy relationship with Him through Jesus. We can read in the Bible about how the ONE Story will tie up its last loose ends and those who believed in God and followed His ways will enjoy unbroken relationship with Him for eternity, but that moment has not yet arrived. Therefore, God's ONE Story is still being played out, even if its script of the beliefs and conduct of its participants has already been written!

This means that you can have your part to play in God's story. As we have seen, God created you so that He and you could share in His love and enjoy relationship with one another; that's why He bothered creating anything at all. But you, like all humans, have been separated from God by your sins, transgression, and rebellion. You cannot change that on your own; no matter how much good you try to do, it cannot undo the transgressions you have committed. While separated from God, you tend to rebel more and more, seeking satisfaction in things of this world that cannot really satisfy and will ultimately perish. If you die in that condition, it is too late; you are separated from God, and you will remain separated from God eternally.

That is not what God wanted. Ever since man rebelled against God, God has been working to rebuild relationships with him. This story culminates in God the Son taking on flesh, bridging that wide gap between God and man, in love giving of Himself so that you could be reconciled back to God.

That invitation to be restored back into a right relationship with God through Jesus is still extended to you. Since God loves you, He does not force that relationship on you; you must be willing to accept it. You do so by no longer trusting in yourself, your culture, the world around you, but in Jesus as YHWH (Acts 16:16). You declare that Jesus is the Christ, the Son of God (Romans 10:9–10). You decide to change your heart and mind, no longer to think, feel, and act like you once did, but to learn to think, feel, and act like Jesus did (Acts 2:38). You then submit to being immersed in water for the remission of your sins to receive the forgiveness that comes through Jesus' blood, being joined with Christ in a spiritual death and resurrection (Acts 2:38, Romans 6:3–7).

Then you begin what the Hebrew author describes as "the race that is set before us" (Hebrews 12:1). That is, living lives that glorify God, becoming more like Jesus in the way we think, feel, and act, reflecting the fruit of the Spirit and less of the works of the flesh. Temptations to sin will still beset you, but you can look toward Jesus the Author and Perfecter of your faith and can receive encouragement from all the heroes of faith that came before you (Hebrews 12:1–2). They are not really completely dead; they are alive in spirit, waiting the resurrection, and the Hebrew author invites us to imagine all of them cheering us on as we seek to continue God's story and advance His Kingdom and His purposes in our lives. But you should not imagine that you run this race on your own. You also begin sharing your life with others who believe in Jesus and trust in Him in a local congregation of His people. You develop relationships not just with God but also with fellow Christians, strengthening them while you receive strengthening. In so doing you receive a foretaste of the joy that we all look forward to experiencing in the resurrection when we are completely united with the Triune God and one another in unbroken relationship.

The choice is yours. God wants to enjoy relationship with you and wants you to take on your part in the ONE Eternal Story. I encourage you to do so and join others that seek to do the same!

Questions for Discussion

1. What was God's intention for the creation He made?

2. What went wrong in the creation? How far did man fall?

3. How did God begin to restore His relationship with mankind?

4. Why did God establish a relationship with Israel?

5. What are the connections between the events of Genesis and God's relationship with Israel and the work of Jesus and the establishment of His Kingdom?

6. What will happen on the final day of this creation?

7. How does the ONE Story connect from beginning to end?

8. Do we have a part in God's ONE Story? How can we accomplish that role?

www.ingramcontent.com/pod-product-compliance
Lightning Source LLC
Chambersburg PA
CBHW040322050426
42453CB00017B/2438